Original title:
The Starlit Frost

Author: Paulina Pähkel
ISBN HARDBACK: 978-9916-79-573-6
ISBN PAPERBACK: 978-9916-79-574-3
ISBN EBOOK: 978-9916-79-575-0

Starlight Kisses Winter’s Edge

Beneath the moonlit sky so bright,
Whispers dance in the pale moonlight.
Snowflakes kiss the frozen ground,
In this magic, peace is found.

Trees adorned with silver lace,
Nature dressed in frozen grace.
Stars twinkle like diamonds rare,
Filling hearts with warmth and care.

The night air crisp, the world aglow,
With every breath, sweet winter's flow.
A gentle hush, the world unfolds,
In starlit dreams, our story holds.

As shadows weave with light's embrace,
We find solace in this space.
Close your eyes and take my hand,
In starlight's glow, together we stand.

Frosted Whispers

Amidst the trees, a quiet sigh,
Frosted whispers drift and fly.
Each flake tells of tales untold,
In frigid nights, dreams unfold.

Crystalline branches shimmer bright,
Wrapping the world in soft white light.
Echoes of laughter linger long,
Nature's pulse, a gentle song.

Snowy blankets hide the earth,
Each moment cloaked in quiet mirth.
In winter's grasp, our spirits soar,
With every gasp, we long for more.

The air is still, the stars align,
In frosted whispers, love will shine.
With every step, we dance like fire,
In this stillness, hearts aspire.

Nightfall's Glittering Mantle

Nightfall drapes a velvet cloak,
Stars ignite, the sky awoke.
Each twinkle tells a story bright,
Glittering dreams take to the night.

The world transforms in shades of blue,
With every pulse, a fresh debut.
Moonbeams casting gentle grace,
Illuminating every face.

Underneath this cosmic theme,
We find solace in the dream.
A glittering mantle, soft and wide,
Where wishes thrive and hearts collide.

Stars are whispers in the dark,
Leading us to love's sweet spark.
In nightfall's arms, we drift away,
With dreams to guide us on our way.

Chasing Twinkles on Ice

Skating on a silver lake,
Twinkles dance with every wake.
Laughter echoes, pure delight,
Chasing stars through winter's night.

Each glide like magic, smooth and free,
Chasing dreams as vast as the sea.
In the chilly air, our spirits rise,
Underneath the vast, dark skies.

Frosty winds, a guiding song,
In this moment, we belong.
Hearts entwined, a tender race,
Chasing twinkles with sweet embrace.

As moonlight plays on frozen glass,
We make memories that will last.
In every spin and every glide,
Chasing joy, our hearts collide.

Luminous Silence

Soft whispers float in the night,
Stars twinkle softly, pure delight.
Each breath held, time stands still,
Wrapped in peace, a tranquil thrill.

Moonlight drapes the world in dreams,
Silent echoes fill the streams.
Gentle shadows dance and play,
In the quiet, hearts convey.

A tender hush, the world at rest,
Wrapped in warmth, we feel most blessed.
Every heartbeat, soft and slow,
In luminous silence, love can grow.

Beneath the stars, a fleeting glance,
Connection found in quiet dance.
In hushed tones, our spirits soar,
Luminous silence, forevermore.

Frostbite Serenade

The bitter air whispers around,
With frosty fingers, it unwound.
Snowflakes fall with a gentle grace,
Nature's dance in this frozen place.

Each breath is visible, a puff of white,
The world transformed in shimmering light.
Underneath the starry veil,
This frostbitten night tells a tale.

Hoarfrost clings to branches bare,
A serenade fills the icy air.
Crystal shards twinkle and gleam,
In this winter’s magic dream.

With every crunch beneath our feet,
The melody of cold is sweet.
Frostbite whispers, soft and sly,
In the stillness, we learn to fly.

Frozen Lullaby

The night is soft, a blanket spun,
In frosty dreams, we come undone.
Snowflakes kiss our sleepy eyes,
In this realm where silence lies.

Whispers of winter wrap us tight,
Hushing worries, banishing fright.
A lullaby sung by the trees,
In the still, a gentle breeze.

Crystals spark in moon's embrace,
Time slips by in this sacred space.
Each twinkle sends us far away,
To a land where worries fade.

Let the chill envelop our hearts,
As the frosty magic starts.
In dreams of snow and silver light,
We find solace in this night.

Celestial Glow upon the Snow

Underneath a canvas vast,
Celestial bodies gleam and cast.
Their glow upon the snow below,
A radiant dance, a gentle flow.

Each star a witness, bright and bold,
Telling secrets, tales of old.
In the silence, worlds collide,
As dreams awaken, hearts abide.

The snow reflects the sky's embrace,
A mirror of the stars' own grace.
In this harmony, souls connect,
Lost in wonder, we reflect.

A celestial glow, serene and pure,
In winter's grasp, we feel secure.
Through the night, we roam and tread,
In a world where magic's led.

Winter’s Glistening Sonnet

Snowflakes dance down from the sky,
Whispers of frost, a gentle sigh.
Trees wear coats of silver white,
In winter's grasp, the world feels right.

Crystals glimmer on every branch,
Nature holds its frozen trance.
Silent nights with stars so bright,
Wrapped in blankets, hearts take flight.

Footprints mark the quiet ground,
In this stillness, peace is found.
The moon beams down its tender glow,
In winter's embrace, love does grow.

Cosmic Bows Over Frosted Fields

Morning breaks with golden rays,
A tapestry in frosty maze.
Fields adorned in white and blue,
Whispers tell of dreams anew.

Bows of light dance on the dew,
Nature's brush, a vibrant hue.
Every flake a story told,
In the air, crisp wonders unfold.

Shadows stretch as sun ascends,
Moments linger, time suspends.
With each step, a warmth ignites,
In the chill, the heart delights.

Celestial Winks in a Chilly Veil

Stars peek through the velvet night,
Whispers of warmth, a soft twilight.
With each breath, a frosty mist,
Cold kisses in a lover's tryst.

A silver path beneath the moon,
Nature hums a gentle tune.
Winks of light in the dark expanse,
Invite the soul to take a chance.

Glimmers play on barren trees,
Carried softly on winter's breeze.
Under this spell, hearts find reprieve,
In chilly veils, we dare believe.

This Magic Night in Frigid Light

Beneath the stars, a magic night,
The world aglow with pure delight.
Each breath lingers, crisp and clear,
In this moment, love is near.

Frosted branches sway so low,
Whispers of winter gently flow.
With a heart so warm, we share,
In this embrace, we are laid bare.

Fireflies dance in shimmering air,
A festive glow, a tender stare.
Wrapped in wonder, laughter bright,
This magic night, our hearts take flight.

Mysterious Glades Under the Frozen Glow

In the glades where shadows creep,
Winter whispers secrets deep.
Frosted branches touch the night,
Gentle glimmers, soft and bright.

Moonlight dances on the ground,
Silent echoes, magic found.
Snowflakes swirl in twirling grace,
Nature’s beauty in this space.

Ancient trees in silent watch,
Time has paused, the world a blotch.
Mysterious paths call my name,
In this glade, I feel the same.

Underneath the frozen glow,
Wonders wait, they ebb and flow.
Heartbeats match the starry sky,
In this realm, I long to fly.

Night will fade and light will break,
Dreams awaken, softly shake.
In the glades, I lose my way,
Yet with dawn, I find the day.

Dusk's Crystal Kiss on a Dreamy Expanse

At dusk when colors softly blend,
The sky becomes a cherished friend.
A crystal kiss from twilight's cheek,
A moment rare, the heart’s mystique.

Whispers of the evening breeze,
Ride the shadows through the trees.
Each star emerges one by one,
A gentle glow, the day is done.

Rippling lakes reflect the hue,
A dreamlike world, so fresh and new.
In this expanse, I feel so free,
Entwined with night’s sweet melody.

Clouds drift lazily, rich and bold,
Their stories in the dusk unfold.
A serenade for souls that roam,
In twilight's arms, we find our home.

As darkness wraps the world in peace,
The worries of the day release.
In this moment, I’m alive,
Dusk's crystal kiss, my heart's archive.

The Silent Gleam of Winter

Quiet whispers of the snow,
Softly falling, row by row.
Each flake dances in the air,
A glimmered sheen, a lull so rare.

Branches draped in silken white,
Embers fade in waning light.
Footprints shadowed, all is still,
Nature's heart with peaceful thrill.

The moon glows bright in velvety night,
Casting dreams in sparkling light.
Hushed embrace of winter's breath,
Clad in beauty, life finds rest.

Candles flicker, warmth inside,
As winter's tales begin to glide.
Sipping cocoa, hearth aglow,
Chilly winds, a gentle flow.

Draped in blankets, lost in thought,
The world outside, a treasure sought.
In winter’s grasp, we find our gleam,
A silent night, a timeless dream.

Radiant Chill

Crystals twinkle on the ground,
Nature's magic all around.
Breath of ice, a silver thread,
A tranquil hush, where dreams are fed.

Branches sway with silent grace,
Underneath the frosted lace.
Stars above in darkened skies,
Whisper secrets, softly sighs.

Every moment, still and sweet,
Echoes gently in the street.
Fingers numb, yet hearts are warm,
In winter's chill, we find our charm.

Pine trees wear their snowy crowns,
Softened edges, muted sounds.
A brisk embrace, a fleeting thrill,
In the quiet, time stands still.

As night descends, the world aglow,
In radiant chill, we come to know.
With every breath, a story spun,
In the dance of snow, we are one.

Fables of the Frosted Night

Underneath the twinkling stars,
Whispers weave like ancient bars.
Fables told of ice and fire,
Dreams that linger, hearts inspire.

Shadows flicker, stories told,
In the chill, the brave and bold.
Winter's breath, a tale to share,
Of love and loss, a timeless care.

Frosted leaves on silent ground,
Echoes of the past abound.
Murmurs of the moonlit glow,
Guide us where the ancients go.

With every step, a trace of lore,
Footprints etched forevermore.
In the night, a magic spun,
Fables whisper, we are one.

Beneath the snow, our dreams take flight,
In the heart of the frosted night.
Through every story, ice and flame,
We find a world but never the same.

Dreaming in Diamond Frost

Morning light on icy panes,
Nature’s jewels, soft refrains.
Sparkling dreams in winter’s clutch,
A world transformed by nature's touch.

In the stillness, whispers drift,
Silent echoes, spirits lift.
Frosted patterns lace the trees,
Nature's art, a gentle breeze.

Each flake tells a tale anew,
Of distant lands and skies so blue.
Crystal visions, dreams take form,
In the cold, a heart so warm.

Embers glow from hearths within,
Amidst the frost, our hopes begin.
Wrap me in this chilly light,
Dreaming deeply through the night.

Golden rays through icy mist,
In this wonderland, we exist.
Diamond frost, where magic glows,
Dreams unfold as winter flows.

Moonbeams Tracing Patterns in the Ice

Moonlight spills on frozen streams,
Painting dreams in silvery beams.
Whispers of light, a quiet dance,
Nature's artistry, a fleeting chance.

Each shimmer tells a story bright,
Of winter shadows kissed by light.
Glimmers weave through crystalline air,
Chasing secrets hidden with care.

Ice reflects the night so clear,
Echoes of magic linger near.
While owls hoot in the stillness profound,
Moonbeams trace where wonder is found.

Beneath the sky a canvas unfolds,
In silver hues, the world beholds.
As night deepens, the patterns grow,
A ballet of frost, in its own flow.

Radiance Adrift in Frosty Silence

In silence draped, a glow persists,
Radiance dances in icy mists.
Stars blink brightly in velvet dark,
While crisp air carries a gentle spark.

Frosted breaths weave through the night,
Each inhale a whisper, soft and light.
Cloaked in white, the world stands still,
As time surrenders to winter's chill.

Every crystal holds a spark divine,
Reflecting dreams that intertwine.
In this tranquil realm of snow and ice,
The heart finds peace, the soul finds solace.

The moon reigns high in tranquil grace,
Casting shadows, a soothing embrace.
A serenade of glimmers and gleams,
Where silence cradles all our dreams.

A Tapestry of Stars and Snow

Beneath a quilt of shimmering white,
Stars twinkle softly, a celestial sight.
Threads of frost weave through the night,
A tapestry born from heaven's light.

Each flake a story, unique and true,
Kissed by the heavens, a world anew.
Starlight glistens on a powdery bed,
Painting visions where angels tread.

The night whispers secrets, serene and bold,
In the embrace of winter, stories unfold.
Silent pathways glimmer as we roam,
In this enchanted realm, we find our home.

As constellations guide our way,
The fabric of night leads us to play.
A dance of joy in the softest glow,
In a world alive with winter's snow.

Luminescent Frost Over Sleeping Pines

Tall pines slumber beneath the frost,
In their stillness, no moment lost.
Each branch adorned with diamonds bright,
A spectacle born of pure moonlight.

Whispers glide through the frozen trees,
Carried softly by the winter breeze.
Luminous frost wraps the night in peace,
Nature's embrace brings timeless release.

A blanket of white on towering heights,
Kissing the earth in winter bites.
In cushioned quiet, the world feels whole,
While magic wakes the frozen soul.

While shadows stretch as the night draws near,
Each glimmering branch holds a promise dear.
In this realm, where dreams intertwine,
Luminescent frost over sleeping pines.

Icy Breath of the Infinite Sky

The world beneath a frozen mask,
Whispers secrets the wind will ask.
Stars twinkle in the navy deep,
While silent shadows fall asleep.

Clouds drift slowly like a dream,
Carrying whispers from the stream.
Each breath lingers in the cold,
A tale of warmth yet to be told.

Ice crystals dance on fleeting light,
Painting visions of the night.
The universe in frozen grace,
A masterpiece, the stars embrace.

Echoes of the universe roam,
In the chill, we find our home.
Beneath the vast, enchanting dome,
The icy breath weaves our poem.

In the silence, dreams take flight,
On wings of frost, through endless night.
With every sigh of winter's breath,
We celebrate the dance of death.

Catching Stars in a Crystal Chill

Fingers stretch to grasp the glow,
Of distant worlds in the midnight flow.
Every sparkle sings a tune,
Beneath the glimmering, watchful moon.

Icicles hang like frozen tears,
Reflecting whispers of our fears.
But in the dark, hope's embers spark,
Lighting up the endless dark.

With every breath, the air grows bright,
As constellations paint the night.
In this stillness, magic thrives,
While dreams awaken, come alive.

We reach for heavens, icy crown,
As snowflakes fall, without a sound.
Catching stars, a fleeting wish,
Wrapped in nature's tender kiss.

Each moment counts, a jewel rare,
In the chill, our souls lay bare.
We dance among the spectral light,
Catching stars, in crystal night.

Soft Boughs Beneath a Radiant Layer

Beneath the snow, the earth lies still,
Wrapped in warmth against the chill.
Soft boughs cradle the weight of white,
Guardians of the twinkling night.

Branches arch like whispering hands,
Holding secrets from distant lands.
Radiant layers coat the ground,
In this quiet, peace is found.

Footsteps leave a gentle trace,
Carved in nature’s soft embrace.
Every flake, a story spun,
Tales of winter, life begun.

Light dances on the frozen scene,
As shadows stretch and softly glean.
In this moment, time stands still,
Caught in beauty's tranquil thrill.

The hearth of night invites us near,
Underneath the silver sphere.
Soft boughs hold our dreams in trust,
In this wonder, we find us.

Underneath a Tapestry of Frost

A woven frost, a fleeting dream,
Each layer whispers, soft and serene.
Underneath the shimmering dome,
All is quiet, all is home.

Delicate patterns grace the trees,
Choreographed by winter’s breeze.
Nature’s art, a silent plea,
Inviting us to simply be.

Moonlight casts its gentle glow,
Illuminating paths below.
In this grace, we wander free,
Wrapped in winter's reverie.

Every breath brings forth a spark,
Echoing softly through the dark.
We dance where frost and shadows blend,
In this magic, we transcend.

Beneath this quilt, our hearts engage,
Stitched with memories, page by page.
Underneath the glistening frost,
We find the love that cannot be lost.

Diamond Dust Over Silent Meadows

In the hush of dawn's bright hue,
Sparkling light on grass anew,
Nature whispers in the breeze,
Carried soft through swaying trees.

Every blade, a twinkling star,
Morning's gift from near and far,
Gentle steps on frosted ground,
Peaceful silence all around.

Clouds drift softly, light as air,
Fleeting moments, chill to bear,
Fields aglow in diamond spark,
Where quiet dreams weave in the dark.

Frosty patterns, pure delight,
Glimmering shards in morning light,
Nature's canvas, vast and grand,
Crafted gently by winter's hand.

As the sun begins to rise,
Color floods the painted skies,
Meadows sing in vibrant hues,
Diamond dreams in morning's muse.

Blushing Skies of Frosty Whispers

As daylight fades with soft embrace,
The sky adorns its blush of grace,
Whispers echo through the trees,
Carried on the winter's breeze.

Peach and lavender collide,
Marking twilight's gentle stride,
Stars awaken, twinkling bright,
In the tender cloak of night.

Frosty breath upon the air,
Nature glistens, wondrous, rare,
Dreams take flight on evening's wing,
In this hushed and sacred spring.

Snowflakes dance in swirling flight,
Kissing ground with purest white,
Each a tale from heaven spun,
Merging with the setting sun.

As shadows deepen, hearts will yearn,
For the warmth that spring will earn,
Yet in the chill we find our peace,
In blushing skies, our worries cease.

Tranquil Lights Beneath the Icy Firmament

Underneath the starry dome,
In the vastness, we call home,
Whispers linger in the night,
Breaths of wonder, pure delight.

Icy tendrils hold the glow,
With every twinkle, spirits flow,
Nature's lullaby, so sweet,
Guides us through the soft retreat.

Crystalline dreams in silver hues,
Wrapped in silence, hearts infused,
Beneath the moon's soft, watchful gaze,
We bask in its gentle blaze.

Time stands still in this embrace,
Infinite peace in endless space,
The firmament, a canvas wide,
Where each star, our hopes collide.

Moments fleeting, cherished, dear,
So we hold each glimmer near,
In tranquil lights, we find our way,
Guided softly, night to day.

Glacial Glimmers Under Velvet Canopies

Beneath the velvet sky, we roam,
Where glacial glimmers find a home,
Trees adorned in frost's embrace,
Nature's beauty sings of grace.

Each branch drips with winter's breath,
A life preserved, yet hinted death,
Where shadows dance in moonlit beams,
And whispers weave through frozen dreams.

The night unfolds in twilight's glow,
As glimmers spark on fields of snow,
Under canopies of night,
Every moment, pure delight.

Footprints trace the path we tread,
Silent echoes where we've led,
Joining with the stars above,
In the quiet, feel the love.

Together, lost in winter's grace,
In this stillness, we find our place,
Glacial glimmers, soft and bright,
Guide our hearts through the night.

The Secret of Sparkling Nocturne

Beneath the velvet sky so wide,
Whispers of stars begin to glide.
Each twinkle hides a tale untold,
Of ancient dreams and treasures bold.

A moonlit path the shadows cast,
Where echoes of the night hold fast.
Glimmers dance on a silver stream,
Awakening a silent dream.

In the quiet, secrets sleep,
Amidst the depth of night’s dark keep.
Every sigh of wind reveals,
The hidden truths the darkness steals.

Crickets sing their midnight song,
While shadows stretch, they glide along.
In the stillness, wonders shine,
Tracing arcs of the divine.

A lantern flickers, dim yet bright,
Guiding souls throughout the night.
In this realm where dreams transpire,
The secret dances in the fire.

Luminary Glints in the Hushed Twilight

As day departs and night takes hold,
Twilight whispers, soft and bold.
Stars awaken, gleaming white,
Painting shadows in the night.

A canvas stretched with colors rare,
Dimming sun, the world laid bare.
Amber glints adorn the sky,
Where dreams and wishes dare to fly.

The breeze carries a lullaby,
In every hush, the heavens sigh.
Glints of hope in twilight’s sway,
Guiding hearts who’ve lost their way.

Crimson hues in fading light,
Merge with softening hues of night.
Each moment soft, each breath a gift,
In twilight’s grace, our spirits lift.

The stars align, a cosmic dance,
Inviting hearts to take a chance.
In this hush where secrets dwell,
Glimmers weave their timeless spell.

Frost-kissed Serenade in the Dark

In the stillness, frost takes flight,
Glistening like diamonds in the night.
A serenade both soft and clear,
Whispers of winter drawing near.

Icicles drape with silver grace,
Each one a note in time and space.
The moonlight weaves through trees so bare,
Painting shadows everywhere.

The chilling breath of winter's song,
Echoes softly, whole and strong.
Every flake a whispered prayer,
Floating down with gentle care.

Stars are strewn across the sky,
As frosty winds begin to sigh.
In this stillness, hearts will yearn,
For warmth and solace to return.

With silver gleams on every ground,
In this serenade, peace is found.
Frozen moments, pure and bright,
In the dark, they come to light.

Night's Embrace of Glimmering Ice

Wrapped in night’s soft, gentle fold,
The world lies still, a tale retold.
Glistening ice, a crystal sheen,
Casting dreams where none have been.

Every breath is a shivering sigh,
As stars hang low in the frosted sky.
Glimmers twinkle on frozen streams,
Awakening the heart’s lost dreams.

The chill weaves through the silence deep,
Luring souls into a tranquil sleep.
With every spark, the night reveals,
The secrets that the darkness steals.

Echoes fade in the still of time,
While moonlight bathes the world in rhyme.
In this embrace, hearts intertwine,
Finding warmth in the glimmering line.

Together, lost in night’s allure,
In every spark, the heart feels sure.
Embracing ice, so cold and bright,
We find our peace within the night.

The Frozen Oath

In the silent woods of snow,
Each whisper binds us, soft and low.
Promises made in the twilight's grace,
A vow held close in this tranquil space.

Stars above begin to gleam,
In frozen tales, we weave a dream.
Hearts entwined in winter's breath,
Our love is strong, defying death.

The frost surrounds, a crystal light,
Guiding us through the endless night.
With every flake that drifts from skies,
Our oath remains, where truth complies.

Upon the frost, our footsteps mark,
A journey shared, igniting spark.
The world may chill, but we hold warm,
Together strong, we brave the storm.

In the realm of slumbered rest,
Bound by warmth, we feel the best.
With every heartbeat, closer still,
The frozen oath, our spirits thrill.

Crystalline Echoes

In the glade where shadows play,
Crystalline echoes dance and sway.
Each sound a shimmer, pure delight,
Resonates in the still of night.

Leaves adorned with icy lace,
Nature's whisper, a fleeting trace.
Reflections sparkle in the moon,
Harmony sings a haunting tune.

Through drifting snow, the silence calls,
Listen closely, as magic falls.
Every note, a twinkling star,
Carried softly, near and far.

In this realm of winter's bliss,
I find my heart in every kiss.
A world transformed, the frost ignites,
Crystalline echoes, winter's rights.

Hold this moment, let it be,
Bound in time, just you and me.
Together, we’ll chase away the cold,
In crystalline echoes, stories told.

Frost-tinged Reflections

Mirrored lakes in frosty dawn,
Capture whispers from the lawn.
Each ripple dances with the sky,
Frost-tinged reflections, spirits fly.

Branches heavy, painted white,
Glimmers glow, a wondrous sight.
In stillness found, our spirits soar,
A world adorned, we can't ignore.

Frost-kissed petals, nature's art,
Touch the beauty of the heart.
With every glance, the stories weave,
In silent peace, we dare believe.

Time unfolds in icy streams,
Carried forth like fleeting dreams.
In this moment, we embrace,
Frost-tinged bliss, a sweet embrace.

We share the warmth, the chilling air,
In each reflection, love laid bare.
Together, we face the morn anew,
Frost-tinged reflections, me and you.

Embrace of the Chilled Moon

Underneath the chilled moon's light,
We wander hand in hand, in flight.
Stars encircle us like a dream,
In the stillness, hearts gleam.

Snowflakes fall like whispered sighs,
Dancing gently from the skies.
Each breath we take, a frosty song,
In this embrace, we both belong.

The night wraps us in cool caress,
In this moment, we find our rest.
The moon above, our guiding flame,
Filling our souls with tender aim.

In shadows cast by silver glow,
Secrets shared through the falling snow.
Together lost in winter's grace,
The chilled moon's warmth, our favorite place.

As dawn approaches, a distant hue,
We cling to dreams, both old and new.
Embraced forever, with love's delight,
Under the moon, we share the night.

Crystals in the Night

In the stillness of the night,
Crystals twinkle, pure and bright.
Whispers float on the cool breeze,
Holding secrets, hearts at ease.

Moonlight dances on the ground,
Shadows play, and dreams abound.
Magic weaves through every beam,
In this world, we softly dream.

Stars ignited in the sky,
Echoes of a silent sigh.
Each one holds a tale untold,
In the dark, their glories unfold.

As the night begins to fade,
Nature's beauty, softly laid.
Crystals shimmer, then depart,
Leaving warmth within the heart.

Dreamscapes in Blue

Endless skies of ocean hue,
Whispers drift, and hopes renew.
Clouds like dreams, they float and sway,
In this beautiful display.

Gentle waves kiss sandy shores,
Heartbeat echoes, evermore.
In this blue, serenity,
Cradles souls, sets them free.

Misty morning, soft and bright,
Dawning shores embrace the light.
Every hue sings peace and grace,
Time suspended in this place.

In our dreams, we wander wide,
With the tides, we ebb and glide.
Blue horizons let us soar,
In this realm forevermore.

Whispers of the Frozen Sky

Snowflakes dance on whispered winds,
Nature's hush as winter begins.
Stars shine cold in azure deep,
In the night, our secrets keep.

Frosty breaths in chilled embrace,
Time stands still in this vast space.
Crystal clear, the air is light,
Holding dreams in frozen night.

Silence wrapped in snowy white,
Every flake a quiet flight.
In the stillness, wonders bloom,
Whispers weave through winter's gloom.

When the dawn begins to glow,
Magic under blankets slow.
In these whispers, hearts will find,
Love that's nurtured, warm and kind.

Shimmering Veil of Winter

Veils of white adorn the pines,
Shimmering in the soft moonshine.
Footsteps crunch on frosty ground,
Every moment, joy is found.

In the hush of winter's breath,
Life transforms, defeating death.
Crisp air carries laughter clear,
Echoes far for all to hear.

Every branch a crystal tale,
Nature whispers without fail.
Wrapped in warmth, we gather tight,
Lost in dreams of snowy night.

Beneath the stars, we intertwine,
Hearts aglow, pure and divine.
In the shimmering, timeless glow,
Winter's wonders softly flow.

Whispers of Winter Night

The snowflakes dance upon the air,
Silent secrets everywhere,
Moonlight glimmers on the frost,
In this beauty, we find what’s lost.

A hush descends, the world at rest,
Nature's blanket, softest vest,
Trees like shadows in the glow,
Whispers of winter, sweet and slow.

Stars awaken, twinkling bright,
Guiding dreams through the night,
Footprints vanish, time stands still,
In this wonder, hearts refill.

Breath like clouds in crisp, clear air,
Each moment cherished, true and rare,
Embrace the chill, the tranquil sound,
Where whispers of night freely abound.

In the silence, warmth we find,
Binding memories, intertwined,
A soft sigh in the peaceful night,
Where winter's whispers feel just right.

Celestial Crystals

In the heavens, starlight gleams,
A tapestry of twinkling dreams,
Crystals of light, like jewels scattered,
Where cosmic secrets are gently chattered.

Galaxies swirl in a dance divine,
Each one a spark, a whispered sign,
Feel the pull of the infinite sky,
As stardust glimmers on the sigh.

Nebulas bloom in colors bright,
Painting the canvas of the night,
Celestial waters of midnight sea,
Reflecting who we long to be.

Through the quiet and vast expanse,
We find hope in the stars' dance,
Crystals of wisdom, shining clear,
In every heart, they draw us near.

Look up high, embrace the glow,
In these wonders, let love flow,
Together we journey, hand in hand,
Under the sky's enchanting strand.

Glimmering Dreams in Ice

Through the frost, a vision glows,
Glimmering dreams, where magic flows,
Ice sculptures, flawless and bright,
Reflecting whispers of softly light.

In frozen realms, our wishes take flight,
Cascading joy in serene delight,
Crystal patterns that twirl and spin,
A symphony where dreams begin.

Each shard a story, timeless, bold,
Capturing memories, tales retold,
Glistening paths in the moon’s embrace,
Where love and warmth find their space.

In this wonder, let go of fears,
For glimmering dreams, we’ll set our gears,
With icy breath upon our lips,
We’ll sail on frost, the world eclipsed.

As night unfolds, let us ignite,
The flame of hope in the winter’s bite,
In the heart of ice, we'll always find,
Glimmering dreams that bridge the mind.

A Tapestry of Stardust

Woven threads of cosmic light,
In every stitch, the stars ignite,
A tapestry, both vast and near,
Where every heartbeat holds us dear.

Each moment captured, woven tight,
A dance of galaxies, pure delight,
Patterns swirl like breezes blown,
In this fabric, love is sown.

The universe sings in vibrant hue,
Through the darkness, life rings true,
Every color, every thread,
Brightly lives where dreams are fed.

In silken shadows, whispers dwell,
Echoes of wishes, tales to tell,
We're bound by the wonders, the paths we choose,
In a tapestry of stardust, we cannot lose.

So weave your wishes, grand and small,
In the arms of starlight, let spirits enthrall,
For in this fabric, forever we'll stay,
A tapestry of stardust, leading the way.

Midnight’s Icy Breath

Whispers of cold fill the night,
Stars twinkle with frosty delight.
Shadows dance under the pale moon,
Hearts beat slow, as time won’t swoon.

Snowflakes fall, soft as a sigh,
Nature’s tingle, a lover's lie.
Brittle branches creak and sway,
Echoes of night gently play.

Winter's veil drapes all around,
Beauty lost in frosty sound.
Moments freeze, yet time stands still,
A silent wonder, a magic thrill.

In the chill, memories linger,
The world wrapped in a frozen finger.
Breath clouds rise, a fleeting ghost,
Treasures cherished, we love the most.

Life finds warmth in the coldest days,
In midnight’s hug, our spirits blaze.
Together we face the icy night,
Forever bound, hearts taking flight.

The Light of a Winter's Dream

Softly falling, the purest snow,
Blanketing earth in a gentle glow.
Each flake dances, fierce yet light,
Whispers of love in the winter's night.

The dawn breaks softly with a smile,
Shimmering beams stretch out a mile.
Dreams etched in morning's embrace,
Hope renews in time's warm grace.

Fires crackle, warmth fills the room,
Embers flicker, dispelling gloom.
A tale unfolds, spun from gold,
In winter's arms, light we hold.

Echoes of laughter bright in the air,
Gathered close, with love we share.
Winter's chill can't touch our hearts,
In this dream, forever our part.

As twilight falls with a soft sigh,
Stars awaken in a deepening sky.
In winter's light, we find our way,
Guided by love, come what may.

Glacial Echoes

In the stillness, whispers glide,
Frozen secrets, worlds collide.
Crystal shadows, reflections beam,
Nature's dance, a silent dream.

Mountains stand in purest white,
Guardians watch through day and night.
Every gust a story told,
Timeless treasures, silent gold.

Frosted branches reaching high,
Breath of winter, soft and nigh.
Echoes pull from ancient past,
In glacial realms, moments last.

Footprints etched in snow so bright,
Each step speaks of pure delight.
Winds carry tales from afar,
In icy realms, we find our star.

As day fades to twilight’s kiss,
Frozen beauty, winter’s bliss.
In the heart of the glacial breath,
Life ignites from the shadow of death.

Radiance upon White

A canvas pure, untouched, serene,
Blanketed dreams in silver sheen.
Sunrise spills across the land,
A radiant brushstroke, nature's hand.

Footsteps crunch on the frosted ground,
Magic twirls, a dance profound.
Light plays tricks upon the ice,
In this stillness, everything's nice.

Sparkling flakes, purest delight,
Twinkling stars in broad daylight.
Nature shimmers, a worthier prize,
Born anew under winter's eyes.

Warmth ignites from hearts so close,
In winter's glow, love matters most.
Memories whisper in woven dreams,
As light flows soft in silver streams.

Hand in hand through the frozen expanse,
In this haven, we find our chance.
Radiance beams through the purest sight,
Finding solace in winter's light.

A Midnight Frost Song

In the hush of night, frost gleams bright,
Whispering secrets, cold as light,
Trees wear crystals, a sparkling crown,
Nature's silence, a softened sound.

Moonlit shadows dance and sway,
Underneath the stars' ballet,
Every breath, a misty sigh,
Embraced by winter's lullaby.

Footsteps crunch on frozen ground,
In this stillness, peace is found,
Warming hearts with every chill,
As frosty air begins to thrill.

A serenade of icy tones,
Echoes through the night alone,
Stars above in their radiant place,
Mark the beauty of winter's grace.

In a world draped soft and white,
Frosted dreams take dreamy flight,
Wrapped in blankets, spirits rise,
Beneath the vast, enchanted skies.

Whispers of the Winter Sky

Skyward flows a silver tale,
Winds that weave a gentle wail,
Clouds like whispers drift and sigh,
In the chill of a winter sky.

Stars like diamonds, twinkle bright,
Over snowflakes in their flight,
Every shimmer tells a story,
Of icy realms and fleeting glory.

Brisk and fresh, the evening air,
Wraps the world with tender care,
Trees and fields in still repose,
Underneath the crystal prose.

With every breath, the night is clear,
Filling hearts with winter's cheer,
Nature's voice, a calming hum,
Songs of silence softly come.

In this moment, magic glows,
As the frosty river flows,
Love and peace entwined in flight,
Whispers lost in winter's night.

Glimmering Shadows on Icy Veils

Shadows glimmer, softly cast,
On icy veils that hold the past,
Frosted dreams like nightingales,
Sing their songs in winter trails.

Beneath a canopy of stars,
The world shines bright, its beauty ours,
Every flake falls like a tear,
Mirroring joy, dispelling fear.

Cold wind carries tales untold,
Of warmth and love in warmth’s hold,
As giants of the night arise,
Shimmering shadows fill the skies.

With every glance, the heart will swell,
In a winter born from spell,
Nature's rhythm, calm and sweet,
In this frozen, fairytale street.

Embracing light in frosty arms,
This winter world of fleeting charms,
Echoes linger, soft and pale,
In glimmering shadows on icy veils.

Celestial Chills Beneath the Moon

Celestial chills weave through the night,
Beneath the moon in silver light,
Each breath a puff of tender air,
Wrapped in winter's gentle care.

Stars align in cosmic dance,
As frosty whispers weave their chance,
Nature holds her breath so still,
While the heart takes in the thrill.

In the quiet, dreams take flight,
Carried gently through the night,
Every echo, soft and low,
Guiding spirits, ebb and flow.

Through the night, a lullaby,
As shadows skitter, moments fly,
Wrapped in warmth of winter's sway,
As we greet the dawn's new day.

In that stillness, magic grows,
A beauty only winter knows,
Celestial cold, a soothing balm,
While beneath the moon, we stay calm.

Frosted Harmony

In the silence of the night,
Whispers weave through trees,
Moonlight dances on the frost,
Nature's calm, a gentle breeze.

Stars reflect on snow-kissed ground,
Echoes of a peaceful tune,
Crickets rest, the world at sleep,
Cradled by the silver moon.

Icicles glisten like a dream,
Timeless beauty in the dark,
Every breath a frosty mist,
Winter's charm leaves its mark.

Branches bow with crystal weight,
Nature's artistry unwinds,
Tender moments, pure and bright,
In these hours, solace finds.

Harmony in quiet grace,
Frozen symphony of light,
Frosted world, a canvas bare,
Resting softly, calm and bright.

Candida Nightfall

As twilight deepens, shadows bloom,
Candles flicker, soft and bright,
Whispers weave through evening air,
Calling forth the hush of night.

Stars awaken, one by one,
In this canvas painted bold,
Dreams take flight in silver hues,
Stories waiting to be told.

Luna's glow, a guiding light,
Caresses all with gentle grace,
Night unfolds its velvet cloak,
Embracing dreams in soft embrace.

As the world slips into peace,
Shadows play with soft delight,
Candida whispers through the trees,
Enchanting every heart tonight.

Wrapped in stillness, find your way,
In the depths of nightfall's charm,
Where every breath is filled with hope,
And every heart can feel its calm.

Shimmering Veil

Morning light through curtains flows,
Gentle hues of golden grace,
Nature's song begins to rise,
Waking dreams from slumber's place.

A shimmering veil upon the field,
Dewdrops glisten one by one,
Whispers of the dawn unfold,
Heralding the day begun.

Butterflies dance on the breeze,
Color spills from petals fair,
Life awakens in a whirl,
Joy is found in fragrant air.

Sunlight warms the world anew,
Casting shadows, soft and light,
Every corner comes alive,
Bathed in warmth, a pure delight.

Shimmering veil of morning glow,
Wraps the earth in tender care,
Inviting hearts to find their song,
And greet the day that's waiting there.

Spellbinding Winter Whispers

In the stillness, winter speaks,
Softly, like a gentle breeze,
Snowflakes swirl in magic dance,
Frosting trees with quiet ease.

Footsteps crunch on icy paths,
Echoes of a world asleep,
Winter whispers tales of old,
Secrets hidden, dreams to keep.

Branches laden, bows of white,
Nature's beauty, purest sight,
Every flake a work of art,
Crafted in the still of night.

Around the fire, hearts stay warm,
Stories shared beneath the glow,
Spellbinding fantasies arise,
As outside, soft winds blow.

Winter's magic woven tight,
Tales of wonder, soft and bright,
In the quiet, souls will find,
Whispers of the season's light.

Night’s Frozen Ballet

The moonlight shimmers on the snow,
A silent dance, a graceful show.
Whispers of night in chilly air,
Nature's art, beyond compare.

Snowflakes twirl, a soft embrace,
Each one unique, a fleeting trace.
In the stillness, magic unfolds,
A timeless tale that winter holds.

Trees in white, their branches bare,
Echoes of dreams, spun everywhere.
As shadows waltz across the land,
A frozen world, so grand, so planned.

Stars above, like diamonds bright,
Watching over the silent night.
A symphony of cold and light,
In this enchanted, frosty sight.

As dawn approaches, the silence breaks,
The ballet fades as daylight wakes.
Yet in our hearts, it lingers still,
The night’s ballet, a wondrous thrill.

Aurora’s Frosted Glow

In the dark, a shimmer flows,
Beneath the sky, where beauty grows.
Colors dance, a swirling sea,
Aurora's light, wild and free.

Frozen whispers in gentle hues,
Celestial tapestries and muse.
Night's canvas brushed with grace,
Enchanting dreams, we all chase.

With every shift, the sky ignites,
A rhythmic pulse of dazzling lights.
Nature’s magic, bold and bright,
Guiding souls through the winter night.

The icy winds carry secrets old,
Tales of legends and visions told.
Beneath this glow, we stand in awe,
Captivated by the beauty's law.

As morning comes and colors fade,
Memories of brilliance won't invade.
For in our hearts, the vision stays,
A cherished moment through life’s maze.

Stars in Frigid Air

Above, the stars begin to glow,
In the silence, soft and slow.
Each twinkle tells a story lost,
Of ancient nights and dreams embossed.

The air is crisp, a chill ignites,
Starlight dances, shimmering heights.
Wishing wells of hope reside,
In the galaxy's endless tide.

Whispers of the cosmos call,
In this quiet, we feel it all.
Connection found in whispered light,
Guiding travelers through the night.

Frosted breath in the still night's gasp,
Holding moments in a frozen clasp.
As dreams swirl in the chilly air,
Stars remind us of love and care.

As dawn's first light begins to creep,
The stars fade, into shadows deep.
Yet in our hearts, they brightly gleam,
A memory of our midnight dream.

Glacial Radiance

Among the peaks, where silence reigns,
Glacial beauty, nature's chains.
Ice and snow, a breathtaking sight,
Bathed in ethereal, quiet light.

Crevasses deep, like secrets kept,
A canvas vast where silence wept.
In the stillness, whispers grow,
Of ancient tales and rivers’ flow.

Icicles hang in fragile grace,
Glistening chandeliers in time's embrace.
Nature's artistry, stark and bold,
In winter's heart, stories unfold.

The chill bites, but warmth we seek,
In the frost, our spirits speak.
Beneath the cold, a fire burns bright,
With glacial radiance, pure delight.

As twilight falls, the world stands still,
With icy crowns, we dream and thrill.
For even in winter's frozen glow,
Life's pulse lingers beneath the snow.

Shards of Light in the Cold

In winter's grip, the dawn breaks clear,
Shards of light, like crystal, appear.
Each ray a whisper, soft and bright,
Chasing shadows, igniting the night.

Beneath the frost, the earth holds tight,
Silent secrets, cloaked in white.
As sunbeams dance on frozen streams,
They weave together our waking dreams.

A gentle breeze stirs through the trees,
Bringing warmth and a touch of ease.
The world awakens, colors collide,
In the heart of cold, hope will abide.

From every branch, a glint, a shine,
Nature's jewels, a pure design.
Resilient beauty, bold and bright,
In winter's arms, we find our light.

So let us gather, hearts aligned,
In shards of light, our paths entwined.
Together we stand, through the strife,
Embracing the warmth, the gift of life.

Icicles of Eternal Night

Underneath the moon's pale glow,
Icicles hang, a frozen row.
Silent sentinels, sharp and clear,
Guarding secrets the night held dear.

Each drop of dew, a crystal tear,
Whispers of dreams that disappear.
In shadows deep, where no light creeps,
The heart of winter alone keeps.

Isolated, the cold winds sigh,
A haunting tune, a distant cry.
Yet in the chill, there lies a spark,
A pulse of warmth in the dark.

Stars above in velvet skies,
Glimmer softly, as the night dies.
Echoes linger, a timeless flight,
Amidst the icicles of eternal night.

Embrace the stillness, breathe it in,
In the silence, new dreams begin.
For in the cold, there's magic found,
As heartbeats echo, soft and profound.

Glittering Dreams in the Cold

Amid the snow, dreams softly twine,
Glittering thoughts like stars that shine.
Each flake that falls, a wish set free,
In the quiet night, we long to be.

Frozen landscapes, pure and vast,
Whispers of futures tangled in the past.
We trace our hopes in the frost-kissed air,
With every heartbeat, a wish laid bare.

In moonlit glades where shadows play,
Glittering dreams drift, finding their way.
Beneath the ice, a fire burns bright,
Illuminating paths, guiding the night.

Softly we gather, bonds entwined,
Holding each other, souls defined.
For in this cold, there's warmth to find,
A tapestry woven, heart and mind.

So let us dream beneath the stars,
Finding solace in the quiet hours.
Together we'll wander, our spirits bold,
Crafting a story where dreams unfold.

A Ballad of Frozen Stars

In the silence of the winter's night,
Frozen stars shine, a celestial light.
They sing of journeys vast and wide,
A ballad of dreams where hopes reside.

Each twinkling note, a memory spun,
Threads of the past, the battles won.
In the stillness, our wishes soar,
Painting the sky, forever more.

Through icy winds and snowy peaks,
The heart of winter softly speaks.
Whispered songs of old retold,
A tapestry woven of silver and gold.

So gather round, hearts intertwined,
Embrace the warmth our spirits find.
For in this dance of frozen stars,
Lies the promise of who we are.

Let the night cradle our hopes so dear,
As we chase dreams without fear.
In the arms of winter, we will find,
A ballad of love, forever kind.

Constellations Caught in Winter's Grasp

Stars flicker bright in the moonlit night,
A tapestry woven of silver and light.
Snowflakes flutter down, soft as a sigh,
Whispers of secrets as time drifts by.

Frost-kissed branches sway under the weight,
Beneath the vast sky, a celestial gate.
Dreams of warm summers linger in air,
Yet winter holds beauty beyond all compare.

Crystals twinkle on surfaces bright,
Painting landscapes in gleaming white.
Under the heavens, hearts become free,
Finding their place in this cosmic sea.

In quiet of night, wonders unfold,
Stories of stardust and journeys untold.
Each moment cherished, a glimpse of the grand,
Constellations caught in winter's soft hand.

Enchanted Mists in the Gleaming Cold

Mists rise softly from the frozen ground,
Whispers of magic in silence abound.
The world wrapped in layers of tender white,
A spellbinding scene in the pale moonlight.

Winds weave through trees, a delicate song,
Notes of the winter, sweet and strong.
Traces of laughter, echoes of cheer,
In enchanted mists, all worries disappear.

Shadows dance lightly with each gentle breeze,
Nature’s ballet aims to please.
Veils of frost shimmer, a delicate lace,
Transforming the world into an ethereal space.

Every breath taken in the bracing air,
Is filled with wonder, a moment rare.
In the gleaming cold, hearts intertwine,
Enchanted mists, a glimpse divine.

Veiled Secrets of the Winter Moon

Underneath the winter moon's gentle glow,
Secrets linger where soft winds blow.
Veils of white blanket the quiet earth,
While dreams awaken, giving thoughts birth.

Shadows retreat from the light's embrace,
Painting the landscape with delicate grace.
The night holds stories, both ancient and new,
Whispers of magic, hidden from view.

Footprints are etched on the glistening snow,
A path of mystery where few dare go.
In the stillness, the heart learns to hear,
The language of winter, both gentle and clear.

Stars twinkle softly in the vast abyss,
Holding the secrets that we dare not miss.
The winter moon smiles, its wisdom in bloom,
Veiled secrets hidden under frost's loom.

Dappled Frost on Wistful Pathways

Morning light breaks through frost-kissed trees,
Dappled patterns that dance with the breeze.
Footsteps crunch softly on pathways entwined,
Memories linger, with nature aligned.

Wistful reflections weave stories untold,
In each glimmer of frost, there's warmth to behold.
The heart feels alive in the chill of the air,
Each moment is precious, a gift we should share.

Trees stand in silence, dressed in their white,
Guardians of secrets in the quiet night.
Under the sky, where dreams find their way,
Dappled frost glimmers, igniting the day.

A tapestry woven of earth and of sky,
In every breath taken, a soft, wistful sigh.
Adventure awaits on these pathways we roam,
Dappled frost beckons, inviting us home.

Frosted Gleams of Dusk

In the twilight's gentle glow,
Frosted whispers start to flow.
Glances of the day retire,
Embers fade, skies lose their fire.

Branches dressed in icy lace,
Nature's calm, serene embrace.
Silence wraps the world around,
In this peace, lost thoughts are found.

Stars appear, a distant dance,
Inviting dreams to take their chance.
The night unfolds its velvet sheet,
Where shadows and the stillness meet.

Cooler winds begin to sigh,
Softly under the vast sky.
Frosted gleams will mark the night,
As day gives in to softly light.

Hope is born in evening's grace,
In the quiet, find your place.
Frosted gleams of dusk will fade,
Yet linger where memories are made.

Moonlit Shivers

Moonlight drapes the world in white,
Shadows dance, embracing night.
Whispers soft as velvet air,
Hold the dreams we long to share.

Stars align with distant tales,
Guiding hearts like whispered trails.
Cold and warmth in soft collide,
In the moon's glow, love won't hide.

Glistening frost on every tree,
Nature's kiss, wild and free.
Captured moments wrapped in glee,
Within the shivers, we feel the key.

The night basks in a silver hue,
Breathless beauty, pure and true.
Dreams take flight on softest wings,
Driven by the joy it brings.

Moonlit shivers guide the soul,
In that light, we feel whole.
Lost in wonder, hearts ignite,
In the magic of the night.

Sparkling Shadows on the Snow

Underneath the winter's glow,
Sparkling shadows dance on snow.
Each flake glimmers in the light,
Whispers of the softest night.

Footprints trace a story clear,
Echoes of what brought us here.
Colors blend in twilight's hush,
In the cold, our spirits rush.

Branches heavy, laden low,
Kissed by frost, they sway and flow.
Time stands still in quiet grace,
Nature's arms, an endless space.

Glistening crystals melt away,
Underneath the break of day.
Memories trapped within the chill,
Embrace the stillness, take your fill.

To the silence, hearts will soar,
In the shadows, find the core.
Sparkling dreams upon the snow,
In this realm, our laughter grows.

Ethereal Chill

Beneath the veil of northern skies,
Ethereal chill, a soft surprise.
Quiet moments thick with pause,
Nature’s breath invites a cause.

Hushed are voices, gentle night,
Stars like diamonds, pure delight.
In the stillness, heartbeats blend,
Magic lingers, dreams suspend.

Winds of winter softly hum,
Whirling whispers, shadows come.
On the ice, reflections glow,
Beneath the moon, the secrets flow.

Frosty air, a tender kiss,
Promises of purest bliss.
In the chill, feel time unwind,
Calling softly to the mind.

Each breath brings a spark to light,
Ethereal chill, a loving night.
Wrapped in wonder, souls unite,
Chasing dreams till morning bright.

Moonlit Feathers on a Crystal Sea

Beneath the glow of silvery beams,
Feathers drift on soft, gentle streams.
Whispers ride on the cool night air,
As dreams unfold without a care.

The tide hums a sweet lullaby,
While stars twinkle in the vast sky.
Each wave dances with a tender grace,
A tranquil moment, a sacred space.

Shadows waltz along the shore,
Carrying secrets of days before.
The moon smiles down in quiet cheer,
Embracing all that gathers near.

In this realm where silences speak,
The heart finds solace, strong yet meek.
Feathers fall like gentle sighs,
Beneath the canvas where magic lies.

With every glimmer on the tide,
The world slows down, no need to hide.
In the moonlit dance, we find our way,
Embraced by night, we choose to stay.

Shattered Diamonds in the Whispering Breeze

Scattered jewels on the ground,
Whispers of the past abound.
Each fragment sparkles in the light,
Echoing dreams of day and night.

The breeze carries tales untold,
Of lovers lost and hearts of gold.
With every gust, memories blend,
In the fragile air, they ascend.

Footprints linger in the sand,
Stories left by fate's own hand.
Reflections dance in morning dew,
As dawn reveals a vibrant hue.

Fragments glint in early sun,
While shadows stretch, the day begun.
A song of hope, a melody,
Whispered softly by the breeze.

Shattered diamonds on the shore,
Remind us of what came before.
In every gleam, a promise lies,
Beneath the vast, unending skies.

The Cool Caress of Nightfall

As daylight fades and shadows grow,
Nightfall sweeps with a gentle flow.
Stars awaken in the sky's embrace,
Whispers of dreams begin to trace.

A cool caress, the moonlight glows,
Painting the world with silver flows.
Crickets sing their evening tune,
While fireflies dance under the moon.

Leaves rustle in a soft refrain,
Cocooning whispers of love's domain.
The air thickens with unspoken lore,
In the hush where our spirits soar.

Time slows down as breath intertwines,
In the night, where everything shines.
As stars twirl in a tranquil sea,
The cool caress sets our hearts free.

Wrapped in the shroud of twilight's grace,
We find a solace, a hidden place.
In the stillness, the world unfolds,
Where secrets linger and love beholds.

Secrets of Chilled Light and Silence

In the depths of night, where shadows play,
Secrets linger, far away.
Chilled light dances on the ground,
While echoes of silence swirl around.

Stars twinkle like distant sighs,
Holding whispers of ancient lies.
Beneath their gaze, we seek and yearn,
For hidden truths that slowly turn.

The moon weaves tales through silver beams,
Stitching together our restless dreams.
In the stillness, hearts begin to speak,
Craving the warmth in the coldest week.

As shadows stretch and time stands still,
Secrets unfold with grace and will.
Each pause holds a precious clue,
In the chilled light where we wander through.

In silence, we find the paths we seek,
Where echoes guide and spirits speak.
Secrets whispered on the night's soft breath,
In the heart of darkness, we embrace depth.

Celestrial Frosting on the Silent World

A blanket white on fields so still,
Stars twinkle softly, night’s sweet thrill.
Frosted edges kiss the trees,
Whispers of magic carried by the breeze.

Moonlight drapes a silver sheet,
Silent wonders, cold and sweet.
Footprints trace a hidden path,
Nature's peace, a soft, warm bath.

Glistening rooftops, crystal light,
Window panes aglow with night.
Each flake tells tales of old,
In this world, serenity unfolds.

Gentle hush in every breath,
Life stands still, escaping death.
Celestrial hands embrace the ground,
In this silence, solace found.

Icy Flora Blooms Beneath the Stars

Beneath the heavens, blooms arise,
Icy petals, jeweled sighs.
Frozen glades in frosty air,
Nature's beauty, beyond compare.

Frost-kissed leaves hold secrets near,
Crytal shapes, a world so clear.
Under moon’s watchful gaze,
Night unfolds in winter’s haze.

Each blossom holds a twinkling light,
Glowing softly in the night.
Whispers dance on chilly winds,
Life in stasis, beauty spins.

Snowflakes fall like dancers' grace,
On Icy flora, they embrace.
In the dark, a hidden bloom,
Breath of winter, sweet perfume.

Stars above, a guiding guide,
Nature’s art, winter’s pride.
In frozen moments, life is bold,
Icy wonders, dreams unfold.

Night’s Enchantment in a Frozen Dance

The moonlight bathes the world in glow,
A frosty touch, a gentle flow.
Night's enchantment weaves a trance,
Branches sway in winter's dance.

Whispers echo through the trees,
A lullaby on the midnight breeze.
Stars shimmer like a distant glance,
Illuminating shadows as they prance.

Snowflakes drift from skies above,
A hush surrounds, a velvet glove.
Frozen dreams in crystal spins,
Nature breathes where silence begins.

Each step crackles, crisp and bright,
In the stillness of the night.
Footprints trace a serene path,
In the dance, let go of wrath.

As evening fades to dawn’s soft light,
Winter’s tale turns to flight.
Night’s enchantment, a fleeting chance,
In frozen beauty, the heart will dance.

Churning Cosmos in Winter’s Caress

In the cosmos, stars align,
Churning whispers, cold divine.
Winter's breath on silent sea,
A tapestry of mystery.

Frigid winds carve through the night,
Painting skies with shimmered light.
Each swirl and twirl, a timeless song,
Echoes in the void, vast and strong.

A dance of ice beneath the moon,
Galaxies hum a distant tune.
Crystals sparkle in starlit grace,
Winter’s caress, a warm embrace.

Nebulas burst in colors bright,
Reflecting on the endless night.
Churning cosmos, vast and wide,
Winter holds the stars as guide.

Through the cold, a spark ignites,
Illuminating endless flights.
In winter’s grip, dreams set free,
Churning cosmos, find the key.

Glistening Echoes of a Shimmering Night

Stars whisper secrets upon the breeze,
Moonlight cascades through the swaying trees.
Every shadow dances, a joyous ballet,
While silence cradles the close of the day.

Soft glimmers twinkle on ice-covered ground,
The heart of the night beats a soft, sweet sound.
With every heartbeat the world feels alive,
Amidst the glow, dreams and wishes arrive.

In the cool embrace of the deep, dark sky,
Memories glitter as hours drift by.
Each moment a treasure, too precious to lose,
In glistening echoes, the heart finds its muse.

The night wraps around like a silken shawl,
While the stars behold each whispering call.
Glistening echoes of love linger near,
A shimmering night, pure magic, sincere.

We sail through the heavens, with wonder and grace,
The universe beckons, our dreams interlace.
In the shimmering night, we whisper our dreams,
In glistening echoes, all is as it seems.

Frigid Lullabies Under Cosmic Glow

The night beckons softly with frosty embrace,
In the stillness of winter, we find our place.
Gentle lullabies drift on the air,
Cradled by starlight, a moment to share.

Silent blankets of snow cover the ground,
While the universe hums a harmonious sound.
Frigid whispers curl in the biting cold,
Painting each breath with a shimmer of gold.

Floating through darkness, constellations sing,
A symphony woven with hope and with spring.
Frigid lullabies cradling our dreams,
Under cosmic glow, everything gleams.

In the heart of the night, calm waters lie still,
As the world drifts gently, the stars seem to thrill.
Pale moonbeams flicker on frosty white shrouls,
Wrapping us tightly in vibrant night owls.

Under the vastness, our spirits take flight,
Guided by starlight, we dance through the night.
Frigid lullabies weave tales of delight,
In the cosmic glow, all fears take their flight.

Celestial Frost on the Breath of Night

Whispers of frost blanket rooftops so bright,
Celestial dances in the heart of the night.
Stars twinkle softly, a celestial array,
While blankets of silver kiss shadows at play.

The chill in the air brings a magical hum,
As nature awaits for the morning to come.
Each breath is a cloud in this crisp, starry glow,
Celestial frost, with a delicate flow.

Night blooms with wonders, wrapped up in stillness,
While frost-kissed petals exude their sweet brilliance.
In the silence profound, the cosmos aligns,
Sending shimmering visions through infinite signs.

A tapestry woven with dreams and with light,
Unveiling sweet secrets from day to the night.
Celestial frost weaves the fabric of dreams,
In the breath of the night, infinite love beams.

We traverse through starlight on whispers of air,
With hearts intertwined amidst frost and despair.
Celestial beauty, like music, it sings,
On the breath of the night, hope lifts on its wings.

Radiant Gleams of Winter's Heart

In the quiet of winter, a spark comes alive,
Radiant gleams in the frost do arrive.
Each glimmer a story, whispered and shared,
Illuminating paths for those who have dared.

The firelight flickers, casting shadows so long,
While memories twinkle like notes in a song.
Winter's heart pulsates, wrapped in a quilt,
Of dreams and of laughter, in hope, gently built.

Amidst the cold breath of the darkest of nights,
Radiant gleams promise the dawn's warming lights.
With every heartbeat, we honor the past,
Grateful for moments that shimmer and last.

We gather together, our spirits aligned,
Finding warmth in the stories that weave and bind.
Radiant gleams dance around us in cheer,
In the heart of winter, the magic is clear.

Through the chill and the shadows, we rise and we sway,
Embracing the moments that light up the way.
For in every heartbeat, winter shares its art,
In radiant gleams, we find winter's heart.

Beneath the Crystal Dome

Underneath the starlit sky,
Dreams like comets swiftly fly.
Whispers rise like gentle tides,
Beneath the dome where magic hides.

Cold winds dance on winter's breath,
Fleeting shadows wander, death.
But hope ignites with every spark,
A fire's glow within the dark.

Silent echoes fill the night,
Guiding souls with softest light.
We reach up to the fragile space,
Finding joy in icy grace.

Crystals twinkle like the stars,
Embracing dreams from near and far.
In this dome, we come alive,
United here, we gladly thrive.

Beneath this awe, our spirits soar,
In love, we find what we adore.
The crystal gleams, our hearts at peace,
In this embrace, our worries cease.

Dazzle of the Night

The moonlight spills like silver wine,
Across the hills, the stars align.
In shadows deep, the secrets play,
While night unveils its grand ballet.

Whispers glide through velvet air,
Carrying dreams without a care.
A symphony of silence sings,
As magic wraps its tender wings.

The world transforms in midnight's hue,
Embroidery of dark and blue.
Each twinkling light, a story spun,
In dazzle bright, the night is won.

Crickets strum their softest chords,
Nature hums without rewards.
A canvas vast, our hearts ignite,
In every spark, the dazzle bright.

Beneath this sky, we dream anew,
With every breath, our hopes accrue.
Entwined in night’s enchanting flight,
We find our home in the dazzle of light.

Echoes of the Frosted Whisper

In dawns where frost like diamonds lay,
Silent whispers softly sway.
Nature's breath, a chilly song,
Echoes where the shadows throng.

Glimmers dance on crystal streams,
Woven tight in winter's dreams.
Footsteps hush on nature's floor,
With every step, we seek for more.

The pine trees wear their frosty crowns,
Shrouded deep in gleaming gowns.
The echoes call, a serene chase,
In every touch, a warm embrace.

Through valleys wide and mountains high,
The whispers weave their lullaby.
In quiet moments, hearts are stirred,
With every sound, a promise heard.

Wrapped in white, the world holds still,
Each frosted breath, a winter thrill.
We chase the echoes, wild and free,
In frosted whispers, we find the key.

Glacial Wonder

Amidst the peaks where shadows play,
Glaciers whisper tales of gray.
Crystal palaces like dreams unfold,
In their embrace, the stories told.

Cold as ice, yet warm within,
The dance of time, where we begin.
Each crack and crevice holds a sway,
In glacial wonder, lost we lay.

Blue horizons stretch so wide,
Where silence reigns and echoes bide.
Frozen rivers carve their lines,
In every bend, the beauty shines.

The chill brings life, each breath a gift,
In winter's grasp, our spirits lift.
With every glance, the heart grows fonder,
In nature's lap, we roam, we wander.

Gazing at the icy throne,
In solitude, we find our own.
The glacial wonder calls our name,
In frozen realms, we stoke the flame.

Silver Dreams Under the Stars

In stillness, night unfolds its grace,
Whispers of silver in a vast embrace.
Each dream a glimmer, softly bright,
Guiding our hearts in the velvet night.

Beneath the glow of a moonlit sphere,
Wishes take flight, dancing near.
Stars weave stories in the dark,
Igniting hope with a gentle spark.

The sky is painted with cosmic light,
A canvas vast, a pure delight.
Silver threads in the tapestry spun,
Kissing the earth as day is done.

Cradled by night, our spirits soar,
Through the heavens, forever explore.
In dreams of silver, we chase the dawn,
Embracing adventures, free and drawn.

So let us wander where wishes gleam,
In the quiet wonder of a silver dream.
For under stars, our hearts reside,
Together forever, side by side.

Celestial Canvas of Cold

A blanket of ice, the world in still,
Breath of winter, a biting chill.
Stars cast their gaze on the frozen land,
Painting silence with a crystal hand.

Each flake that falls, a story untold,
Secrets of winter in whispers bold.
Sparkling diamonds on branches sway,
In this celestial dance, night turns to day.

Haloed moonbeams cast shadows long,
Nature's orchestra, a wintry song.
Colors muted in the frosty light,
Each breath a puff in the starry night.

A canvas vast, in cold it breathes,
Every drift a heart that weaves.
Through the silence, the world exhales,
In this frozen place, wonder prevails.

As we wander through the icy dreams,
Lost in the beauty of winter's beams.
The canvas cold, yet warm inside,
In celestial magic, we will abide.

Echoes of the Icy Dawn

Awake to whispers of a new day,
Icy tendrils where shadows lay.
Echoes of dawn in hues so pale,
Softly emerging, winter's tale.

Frosted branches, a ballet elite,
Crystals glisten, where night and day meet.
The sun, hesitant, claims the sky,
As echoes of night begin to die.

Footprints trace the silent snow,
A world reborn, where stillness flows.
Each moment held in a breathless chill,
Echoes resonate, the air stands still.

In the fragile light, dreams awaken,
Promises made, and hearts unshaken.
Icy fingers gently touch the ground,
In the echoes of dawn, hope is found.

As the world stirs from its slumbered plight,
We greet the morning, hearts alight.
With each heartbeat, the softest sound,
In the embrace of the icy dawn, unbound.

Twinkles on a Crystal Sea

Under the moon, the sea does twinkle,
Each wave a glimmer, soft as a sprinkle.
Stars reflected in the liquid grace,
A dance of light, a tranquil space.

Whispers of water in gentle sighs,
Breath of the night beneath starlit skies.
The ocean hums its timeless song,
In this crystal world, we belong.

Dancing ripples where dreams collide,
A canvas where the heart confides.
Every twinkle hides a story old,
Of sailors brave and treasures bold.

With every tide, the magic grows,
Mysteries hidden in the ebb and flows.
Reflections shimmer like thoughts set free,
In the twinkles on this crystal sea.

As night unfolds its serene embrace,
We find our peace in this perfect place.
Twinkles guide us, a beacon bright,
Together we journey through the night.

Echoes of Light in Winter's Embrace

In the hush of dusk's soft glow,
Snowflakes twirl like silent dreams.
The world wears a quilt of white,
Where every shadow softly gleams.

Footsteps muffled, whispers near,
Stars peek through the frosty veil.
Each breath forms a fleeting mist,
While night sings a tranquil tale.

Branches bow beneath their load,
Every twig a story told.
Amidst the stillness, spirits rise,
As heartbeats echo, warm and bold.

Lullabies of winter’s grace,
Kissed by moonlight's gentle hand.
In this sacred, frozen space,
We find solace in the land.

Embraced by night's soft caress,
Hope flickers in the dark.
With every twinkle, light reminds,
Winter sings its perfect spark.

Tinkling Stars on a Crystal Canvas

Beneath a sky where secrets weave,
Stars in their shimmering dance conspire.
A canvas stretched, a dreamer's breath,
Each sparkle ignites a pure desire.

Whispers of night in softest tones,
Crafting tales in silver light.
The universe holds its secrets close,
As we wander in pure delight.

Comets streak, like fleeting thoughts,
Tracing paths we oft forget.
In stardust dreams, our wishes flow,
Filling hearts with no regret.

Time stands still in this moment rare,
Each heartbeat echoes in the vast.
On crystal winds, our hopes take flight,
As memories blend with shadows cast.

At dawn, the stars begin to fade,
Yet magic lingers in the air.
To know the night holds wondrous gifts,
Is to embrace the beauty there.

When the Night Sky Dances with Ice

When twilight falls, the world takes pause,
Silvery frost begins to lace.
Stars start to twinkle, soft and bright,
While shadows play in chilly grace.

The moon, a sentinel of night,
Watches over all below.
As chilly breezes stir the trees,
Their frosted breath begins to glow.

Icicles drip from eaves so high,
Each drop a gem, a fleeting glance.
In this hushed and shimmering scene,
The world surrenders to winter's dance.

Colors blend in icy hues,
Painting dreams in gentle light.
As whispers swirl through frosty air,
We find our hearts in sheer delight.

Underneath the starry dome,
Life unfolds in peaceful grace.
With every breath, the world awakes,
In winter's arms, we find our place.

Sparkling Whispers of the Frozen Breeze

Listen close to winter's song,
A melody of crystals bright.
Each note a whisper, soft and clear,
Drifting gently through the night.

Frosty fingers trace the ground,
Glimmering with a tender glow.
In the stillness, magic thrives,
As dreams in icy breath may flow.

Laughter dances with the snow,
Children's joy echoing wide.
While starlit skies weave tales of old,
In every heart, warm hopes abide.

Every flake a work of art,
Unique in its fleeting flight.
Together, they create a quilt,
A masterpiece of pure delight.

So let the world in white embrace,
As sparkling whispers come alive.
In the magic of this frozen breeze,
We find the joy that will survive.

Silvered Nightscapes

In shadows deep, the starlight glows,
A silver sheen on drifting snows.
Whispers of dreams in frosty air,
Soft echoes dance, without a care.

The world transformed, a canvas bright,
Each flake a gem in the cloak of night.
Beneath the moon's delicate gaze,
We wander lost in winter's maze.

Gentle sighs of the midnight breeze,
Carry secrets through the frozen trees.
The silvered landscape, calm and wide,
Holds the magic of the night inside.

A moment caught, time seems to freeze,
Under the stars, we find our peace.
In this realm where silence reigns,
Our hearts find warmth amidst the pains.

As dawn approaches, hues appear,
The silver fades, yet we hold dear.
The nightscape's beauty, etched in soul,
Whispers a truth that makes us whole.

Glacial Moonbeams

Moonlight glimmers on the frozen lake,
A dance of light, a world awake.
Glacial beams, soft touch so rare,
Illuminating beauty dwelling there.

Fragile crystals, like diamonds strewn,
Reflecting secrets of the moon.
With every ripple, stories rise,
In shimmering hues beneath the skies.

A hush cascades upon the ground,
In this stillness, solace found.
Glacial whispers in the night,
Guide our hearts to endless light.

Dreams entwined with frosty air,
In moonbeams' glow, we lay bare.
The serenade of winter's charm,
Wraps us slowly in its warm.

With every glance, a spark ignites,
A promise held in starry nights.
In glacial glow, we find our way,
Where hope survives through bleakest day.

Laughter of the Winter Sky

A burst of joy in cold, crisp air,
Laughter echoes, light and rare.
The winter sky, a lively stage,
Where heartbeats dance with every page.

Above, the clouds like cotton candy,
Twirl and spin, twinkling dandy.
Children's voices, sparkles bright,
Chasing dreams in the fading light.

Snowflakes tumble, a playful flight,
Adventures weave in the frosted night.
Beneath the stars, our hopes alight,
As laughter weaves through sheer delight.

Fireside tales and stories shared,
Warmth surrounds, our hearts prepared.
Together, wrapped in this embrace,
We find our joy in winter's grace.

In every flurry, a giggle spins,
Amidst the chill, the warmth begins.
The laughter of the winter sky,
A melody that will never die.

Fragments of a Frozen Heart

In icy stillness, fragments lie,
Whispers of love that learned to fly.
Frozen moments, caught in time,
Echoes of hearts that felt sublime.

Each shard reflects a memory sweet,
Of fleeting glances, moments fleet.
The cracks tell tales of joy and pain,
Where warmth once bloomed, now silent reign.

Beneath the frost, a longing stirs,
In the quiet, the heart still purrs.
Yearning for sun, for heat to start,
To mend the pieces of a frozen heart.

Snow drifts slowly, watch them fall,
Each flake a prayer, a gentle call.
In the chill, we search the night,
For fragments lost and dreams of light.

Yet in this stillness, hope abounds,
A thawing love in silent sounds.
With spring's embrace, the heart will mend,
As warmth returns and shadows end.

Frosted Dreams in Midnight's Grasp

In whispers soft, the night unfolds,
A tapestry of dreams in winter's hold.
Stars glimmer bright, like frost on grass,
As time slips quietly, moments pass.

The moon bathes all in silver light,
Casting shadows, enchanting the night.
Frozen breath in the crisp, cold air,
Wrapped in stillness, none could compare.

Each flake a wish on this silent sea,
Drifting gently, wild and free.
Memory dances on icy beams,
Awakening our frosted dreams.

Nature rests beneath its icy crown,
In a world of white, no hint of frown.
The heart beats slow, entranced by peace,
In this quiet space, all worries cease.

So linger here, in night's embrace,
Find solace in this frozen place.
Each breath a cloud, each thought a star,
As dreams unravel, near and far.

Silent Sparkle of the Frozen Night

Across the sky, a chill does weave,
The silent sparkles that winter leave.
A symphony of whispers, soft and light,
Dancing softly in the frozen night.

Each crystal glows, a fleeting sight,
Illuminating shadows, pure and bright.
Frigid air wraps around your skin,
Inviting warmth from within.

The world in slumber, deep and wide,
While twinkling stars begin to glide.
With every breath, we trace the glow,
In frozen spaces, our spirits flow.

A serenade of night’s embrace,
In the quiet, we find our place.
Nature's lullaby, a soothing song,
As whispers of winter carry along.

So gaze above at the glistening skies,
A treasure hidden where beauty lies.
In the stillness, hearts unite,
In the silent sparkle of the frozen night.

Ethereal Frost upon the Sleeping Earth

Beneath the stars, a blanket spreads,
Ethereal frost on slumbering beds.
Each blade of grass, a shimmering sight,
Cloaked in diamonds, kissed by night.

The woods are hushed, in muted hues,
Enchanted whispers of frostbitten blues.
Nature dreams in this tranquil state,
Wrapped in stillness, we contemplate.

The echoes of time, frozen in space,
Each moment a delicate, fleeting grace.
In moonlit glow, the shadows play,
As night transforms the night to day.

Awake the earth with a gentle sigh,
As frost melts slowly, bidding goodbye.
Yet in its wake, the beauty is clear,
In the silence, we hold it dear.

So close your eyes, embrace the dream,
Under the frost, life's gentle theme.
In nature's arms, pray to find,
The ethereal frost that soothes the mind.

Luminescent Crystals in the Gloom

In twilight's hush, the crystals gleam,
A soft-lit glow, a silvery dream.
Glimmers dance on shadows' edge,
Nature's treasure, a hidden pledge.

Each glistening gem holds stories untold,
Of transient nights and winter's cold.
With every flicker, a memory sparks,
In the heart of night, where magic hark.

The air is alive with secrets drawn,
In the depth of gloom, a new dawn.
Frigid whispers touch our face,
Bringing warmth to this frozen place.

As we wander through the night's embrace,
Finding solace in this quiet space.
The luminous dance of winter's art,
In chaos, we find a tranquil heart.

So pause and see, in gloom's soft hold,
The beauty of life, a story bold.
In each tiny flicker, our spirits bloom,
With luminescent crystals in the gloom.

Enchanted Nightfall

Stars ignite the velvet sky,
A hush descends, the world feels shy.
Moonlit whispers float on air,
Promises hidden everywhere.

Shadows dance in silver glow,
As fireflies begin to show.
Nature hums a calming tune,
In the cradle of the moon.

Time slows down, breaths intertwine,
Each moment, sacred, feels divine.
Laughter echoes, spirits soar,
In this realm, we are much more.

Hearts unite beneath the night,
Guided by the stars' soft light.
Magic stirs in every glance,
Inviting fate to take a chance.

Embrace the wonder, feel it swell,
In this enchanted night, we dwell.
With every heartbeat, secrets share,
In the stillness, we are bare.

The Dance of Ice and Light

Frosty crystals, glimmering bright,
In a world of pure delight.
Nature's canvas, white and wide,
Where shadows and shimmer collide.

The winds whisper tales of old,
As the icy arms unfold.
Underneath the pale moon's glance,
Everything seems to dance.

Each flake tells a story rare,
Of the chill that fills the air.
Brilliant hues in cold embrace,
Illuminate this frosty space.

Step by step, we find our grace,
In this winter's warm embrace.
With every twirl, our spirits rise,
Mirroring the starry skies.

In this ballet, lost we find,
A harmony of heart and mind.
Together, we'll chase the light,
In the dance of ice, so bright.

Ocean of Frost

Waves of crystal, silence reigns,
A vast expanse of icy chains.
Whispers of the winter seas,
Drifting softly on the breeze.

Blue and white in harmony,
Nature’s cool tapestry.
Underneath the frozen crest,
Lay the secrets, cold and rest.

Glistening shores, a tranquil view,
Where dreams awaken, fresh and new.
Each frosty breeze, a gentle sigh,
Drifting clouds like ships go by.

In the stillness, hearts may roam,
Finding solace, far from home.
In this ocean, vast and wide,
We discover the peace inside.

With every wave, resilience grows,
In the depths where hope still flows.
Ocean of frost, endless and bright,
We’ll embrace the chilling light.

Celestial Dust on Frozen Ground

Glimmers fall like whispers soft,
Celestial dust, a gift aloft.
On frozen earth, the magic lies,
Beneath the vast, enchanting skies.

Sparks of starlight paint the night,
Illuminating shadows tight.
Each grain a wish, a dream to find,
Inventing stories, unconfined.

Ice-kissed landscapes stretch for miles,
Bathed in moonbeams, nature smiles.
Evergreens don their frosted crowns,
Guardians of this sacred ground.

In silent moments, we can hear,
The melody of night, so near.
Eternal whispers, cosmic tune,
In the heart of every rune.

As dawn approaches, colors blend,
Painting horizons, light will send.
Celestial dust to guide our way,
With frozen ground, we'll dance and sway.

Secrets Beneath the Frozen Sky

In the hush of winter's breath,
Whispers float on icy air.
Secrets hidden, dreams entwined,
Beneath the frost, stories share.

Stars weave tales through silent night,
While shadows dances, soft and bright.
Footprints vanish, lost in time,
Echoes linger, steeped in rhyme.

Crystals sparkle on ancient trees,
Nature's art, a silent tease.
Each glimmer holds a tale untold,
In the winter's grip, mysteries unfold.

Beneath the snow, life waits to rise,
Awakening with spring's surprise.
But for now, in frost we dwell,
Holding secrets, magic we tell.

The frozen sky, a canvas pale,
Where every heartbeat leaves a trail.
Beneath this quilt of white and blue,
The world's story whispers anew.

Moonlit Frost

Underneath a silver glow,
Moonlight drapes the world in frost.
Every shadow starts to dance,
In this moment, nothing's lost.

Whispers linger on the breeze,
That carries tales of winter's chill.
Each glimmer sings a soft refrain,
Of secrets hidden, heart's own thrill.

Branches lace the midnight sky,
Cloaked in white, a magical guise.
Frosted whispers call to me,
In this stillness, I can believe.

The frozen ground beneath my feet,
Crackles softly, a gentle beat.
In this dream, the world feels vast,
As moments melt away so fast.

With every glance at the pale orb,
The night's enchantment I absorb.
Moonlit frost, a fleeting kiss,
Captured in this state of bliss.

Vows of Winter Light

In the heart of winter's night,
Promises blend with frosty air.
Crickets hush, the world's at rest,
In the stillness, love lays bare.

Softly glows the fading sun,
As shadows stretch across the land.
Every whisper sings of hope,
In the silence, futures planned.

Crystalline trees stand tall and strong,
Guarding secrets not for long.
In their branches, echoes reign,
Vows of love that touch the plain.

Beneath the heavens, so profound,
The promises in whispers sound.
Each falling flake, a gentle word,
In this frosted world, love is heard.

As the moonlight spills its grace,
I find my heart in winter's embrace.
Every vow, a guiding light,
In the tranquil hush of night.

Enchanted Calm of the Frost

Whispers of a tranquil night,
Wrap the world in silver sheets.
Frosty breezes softly weave,
Through the quiet, nature greets.

The stillness breathes a gentle hymn,
Every flake a note of grace.
In this peace, my spirit soars,
Finding warmth in winter's face.

Frozen lakes, a mirror bright,
Reflecting stars that softly gleam.
Captured moments in the night,
Caught within a dreamer's dream.

With every step on crisp, white ground,
I feel the magic all around.
In this calm, the heart takes flight,
In the embrace of frosty light.

Each breath of air, a chill divine,
In winter's realm, my heart aligns.
Enchanted calm, forever sought,
In icy realms where dreams are wrought.

www.ingramcontent.com/pod-product-compliance
Ingram Content Group UK Ltd.
Pitfield, Milton Keynes, MK11 3LW, UK
UKHW031942151224
452382UK00006B/168

9 789916 795736